Dedication: To everyone who has experienced loss and trauma.

Edited by Tanya Levy

First Paperback edition August 2022

ISBN 978-1-66785-093-1

MosaicsofMary Publications
Georgia, USA
MaryDaugharty.com

Printed by BookBaby
Pennsauken, New Jersey USA
Bookbaby.com

K I T E

Created by Mary Daugharty

Illustrated by Cathy Herring

Soaring up and up that catches
a big wave at seaside.

It dances in the blue air as seagulls and pelicans watch with curiosity.

Until a strong gale rips it out to sea.

It floats on top of the water.

Then, a wave crashed over pulling it under.

And it swam with dolphins,

and whales,

and sea turtles.

Until seaweed attached
to its wooden frame,

and it sank to the ocean floor.

Life and time
flowed all around it.

Seahorses, crabs, and starfish found a home under its naturally shaped roof.

And the kite

was content on the bottom of the ocean floor as it was dancing in the blue air.

Please use this scroll page to express your feelings of loss and trauma as a message to your loved ones that passed away during the Covid-19 Pandemic.

It is an instrument for your creativity.

It is our desire that it brings
peace to your soul.

With love, Mary and Cathy

About the Author

Mary lives in Georgia USA with her husband and their animals. She is a daughter, wife, mom, Nonnie, sister, aunt and friend.

In her childhood, she experienced intense trauma and loss. It took her 50 years to reconcile those traumas and loses.

In May of 2019 she wrote the words that would eventually become this Kite book. At the time she had no idea that a pandemic would upend the world.

It is with utmost sincerity that she wishes that people who have experienced trauma and lost loved ones during this Covid-19 era will find upliftment and comfort from this book.

She can be reached at Marydaugharty.com

About the Artist

Cathy Herring is an artist who specializes in illustrations and paintings. She graduated from Valdosta State University with a B.A. in Art with a concentration in painting and graphic design, and a minor in Sociology.

Cathy is a paraplegic and uses a manual wheelchair to get around. She aims to focus on living her life with gratitude, humor, and creativity.

Cathy lives in Georgia and spends her days as a full-time artist working in her studio along with her pet fish.

She can be contacted at @Cisforcathyart